GW00470651

"

It's not your salary that makes you rich, it's your spending habits

- CHARLES JAFFE

For more guidance on money mindset

and practical tips for better money management:

https://themoneywhisperer.co.uk

For information on how your money personality

impacts your attitude to money:

https://wp.me/p8JdC4-1e8

For questions or suggestions:

emma@themoneywhisperer.co.uk

ISBN: 9781086376937

THE POWER OF YOUR MIND

We are creatures of habit.

Depending on which study you read, between 85% and 95% of the decisions we make on a daily basis are made without any conscious thought. We operate from our subconscious.

Those behaviours you do each day without thinking; they are habits embedded in your subconscious.

If you want to change your relationship with money, you need to identify those habits which aren't helping you to achieve your financial goals.

This spending journal provides a great way to bring your behaviours around how you spend money to your conscious thought.

To use this journal to best effect, write down **everything** you spend money on.

The magic is in the detail; aim to capture where you were, who you were with, what you were doing beforehand, how you were feeling at the time, whether you felt any buyer's remorse afterwards. You get the drift.

Patterns will soon become evident. Maybe you spend out of boredom while you are waiting for the kids to finish sports club. Maybe you overspend on your online grocery shop because you need to get to the minimum spend for free delivery. Maybe you can't resist those sales emails which land in your inbox.

The great thing is that by making your spending a conscious decision, you'll soon start questioning yourself, rather than allowing yourself to operate simply on autopilot.

Enjoy the start of your journey as you change your relationship with money. Starting with getting control of the money flowing out of your life...

Date	Purchase	Cost

Feeling before/after, when, who, why, how

Date	Purchase	Cost

Feeling before/after, when, who, why, how

Date	Purchase	Cost

Feeling before/after, when, who, why, how

Date	Purchase	Cost

Feeling before/after, when, who, why, how

Date	Purchase	Cost

Feeling before/after, when, who, why, how

What have you learnt about your spending habits since you started tracking where your money is going?

Date	Purchase	Cost

Feeling before/after, when, who, why, how

Date	Purchase	Cost

Feeling before/after, when, who, why, how

Date	Purchase	Cost

Feeling before/after, when, who, why, how

Date	Purchase	Cost

Feeling before/after, when, who, why, how

Date	Purchase	Cost

Feeling before/after, when, who, why, how

“

You will never change

your life until you change

something you do daily.

The secret of your success

is found in your daily routine.

- JOHN C. MAXWELL

What elements of your daily routine have changed as a result of the insights you have from using this journal? What else could you change?

Date	Purchase	Cost

Feeling before/after, when, who, why, how

Date	Purchase	Cost

Feeling before/after, when, who, why, how

Date	Purchase	Cost

Feeling before/after, when, who, why, how

Date	Purchase	Cost

Feeling before/after, when, who, why, how

Date	Purchase	Cost

Feeling before/after, when, who, why, how

Go through and mark each item as either a 'want' or a 'need'. I suggest you use a highlighter. What do you notice?

Date	Purchase	Cost

Feeling before/after, when, who, why, how

Date	Purchase	Cost

Feeling before/after, when, who, why, how

Date	Purchase	Cost

Feeling before/after, when, who, why, how

Date	Purchase	Cost

Feeling before/after, when, who, why, how

Date	Purchase	Cost

Feeling before/after, when, who, why, how

Where are your money leaks?

Date	Purchase	Cost

Feeling before/after, when, who, why, how

Date	Purchase	Cost

Feeling before/after, when, who, why, how

Date	Purchase	Cost

Feeling before/after, when, who, why, how

Date	Purchase	Cost

Feeling before/after, when, who, why, how

Date	Purchase	Cost

Feeling before/after, when, who, why, how

Notes

29150976R00038

Printed in Great Britain
by Amazon